water is never still

poems by

JoAnna Scandiffio

Finishing Line Press
Georgetown, Kentucky

water is never still

ACKNOWLEDGMENTS

Grateful acknowledgment is made to the editors of the following journals
in which these poems, sometimes, in an earlier version, first appeared:

Poets 11 Anthology 2016: "water is never still," "flying north of the equator,"
"water stains her hands"
RUNES, A Review of Poetry: "on the day of the dead," "her name is a litany"

Publisher: Leah Huete de Maines
Editor: Christen Kincaid
Cover Art: painting: Annice Jacoby; photograph: Lisa Burlini
Author Photo: Lisa Burlini
Cover Design: Lisa Burlini

Order online: www.finishinglinepress.com
also available on amazon.com

Author inquiries and mail orders:
Finishing Line Press
PO Box 1626
Georgetown, Kentucky 40324
USA

Contents

For my mother's open heart

on the day of the dead

      Papa warns Pedro

            water is never still

      my dress is too short
      I wonder if my mother will notice
            the dead come back as horseflies

      they say

            bougainvillea buzz

      fish are fragrant

      I can't remember my mother's face
      washing my hair she always touched
      faucet water with her wrist
      out of habit
      a ritual is born

            did you know sailors tattoo their names
            not for games but if they slip on a shooting
            star

her name is a litany

of names who have danced a full moon
under too much tequila from a glass filled with roses

maria rosa anna rosa
rosa de fuego passing fire

if you marry an Aztec you
inherit sky and earth

air comes from laughter

fire from falling

a nest of feathers flying

      my mother rocked me to sleep
      to keep the sea
               at arm's length

      my abuela saw
      Cortés through the shutters of her door

      they say

      my brother Pedro walks on shells
      death comes in threes

      why not in pairs

a falcon sings a song   rivers rust

Pedro believes the bones of the dead rise
to play
                        tagalong

sailors pretend a talisman prevents

                wind from kissing their brides

my mother wore her mother's pearls
on the day of her death

my abuela's voice sits in my ear
holding the days before

                my hair unbraided falls

when there is no wind

       sailors count stars

       sometimes they tattoo
       a sweetheart's name or ink

              a blue forest with calling birds

       my mother didn't carry her name or Papa's
       or Pedro's

       on the day she falls back to dust

       I steal
       her lipstick

water is never still

I listen for my mother's voice
at the bottom of a well

I want her to float up orange
so we can rub our hands in the sea

Papa says girls don't have tattoos

Pedro knows they hide them

in places north of the equator
where butterflies run wild

     rum is free

her lipstick is calypso

it burns my lips   I can't wipe it off before
papa notices

I am my mother's voice
catching

         loose ends

sailors at sea hear

their wives' tongues flapping like gulls

they say you can smell death
like an overripe apple forgotten on a table

running off to school I didn't shout

her name three times like a magician
pulling rabbits out of a hat

busy with my books   my hair barrettes
I forgot to clasp her voice to my hand

scribble her words down
like a recipe for milk cake

tres leches cake

all the secrets of the world in one cake

everyone is always stealing
their neighbor's made-up recipe

handing it down as a family heirloom
before the oven cools

everyone knows when sad
eat cake filled with three milks

sugared water is only good for hiccups

if you sleep on a full stomach
                            dreams are interrupted

what else can I steal

on the day

my abuela hangs out the wash
too busy to forget

silver mines are closed today   copper rusts green
the dead linger off moss

Papa shines his shoes so bright
I can see my face in the new moon

                Pedro loses his words

I find them in the back garden
growing like weeds

flying north of the equator

my mother fell from a building without stars

she didn't wear a rabbit's foot or have her name
sewn on a label on the back of her sweater

Papa says you don't have to circle
dates on the calendar
or write everything down

to remember
her jam tastes like candy

without a body   no burial   no place for dancing shoes
her voice singing fire

she could have fallen into a bush
been eaten by a lion   saved by a witch

swallowed by a dolphin

and now will be walking through the door
bringing

store-bought dresses   shoes with cut-out toes
party hats   piñatas as big

as her arms

did you know you can pin down a butterfly

      with colored ink glue and a fine needle

      my brother knows the stars are fixed
      if you get lost

            a hair ribbon will sew your bones together

      you don't have to be a sailor or Cortés

      to have your name

      glow in the dark

a sailor shakes his bones

> to remember what day follows Sunday
> whistles wood to dance a tune he can hold
>
> you can build a nest in the hollow of a trunk
> hide
>
> > moon's vertigo   tales of no return
> > a bride catching cold
> >
> > you can drink sorrow   tell a fib like Pedro
> >
> > crawl into your mother's bed and wait
> >
> > for the tooth fairy to reappear

Montezuma's folly

folly follows my brother like a dog wagging its tail
my father thinks tequila is my mother

Montezuma saw the god Quetzalcoatl in Cortés

this is made-up history   my abuela knows

stories hide
how men scrape the bottom of the sea

did Montezuma give Cortés twenty bowls of gold dust
forty bags of red dye

when I listen to these stories I hear different riddles

      could the sea turn the world upside down
      would Montezuma give away his kingdom

my folly
I believe my mother is a homing pigeon

a sailor's bride waits

counts the days before
then counts backward

adding days she waits

turning the mattress over
and over   until

waiting is
what she remembers

I count stars   wait for my words
to grow feathers   read my school books
cover to cover

so I can learn magic tricks
how to bring the dead back

a bowl of gold dust

magical   if you want to paint a house that glitters
if you need ribbons for your hair   polish on your nails

a bowl of gold dust is not sweet like sugar
nor warm like soup holding my mother's cooling breath

its scent turns sailors feverish   snakes become wizards
stories of Cortes' arrival grow ears   eyes

they say
he is Quetzalcoatl   the feathered serpent

                the north star

                falls out of a sailor's pocket

                the world turns upside down

swimming in books

Cortés comes upon a river of gold
carves his name in a tree

now he will be king of feathers

he maps a circle   marks an X
thinks he won't fall to thunder

my mother floats   like a ghost in my mind

Rosa de fuego Rosa de aqua

I see the night sea in her eyes
laughing at the moon for telling tales

I taste Cortés in the air

he'll give me back
my mother's voice

if I promise not to tell

how many times she counts to a hundred
before my hair turns silk

I'd give all my glass beads
all my school stars
my silver inlaid buttons

for one brushstroke

la corazón

is it true
to save the world

Aztecs fed their gods
human hearts

that were still beating

they say

Montezuma tore the hearts
of young girls

not for the taste of blood

but because he knew the heart tells tales

we let out secrets   my friends and I
like seams in our skirts

*boys whistle
at what they fear*

papa holds the past like a compass
he forgets to notice

I am taller than my mother
I can read

the writing on the wall

a sailor's thirst

for gold

pulls him from his bride before
his seed takes root

sailors sing in sync

when the whale tips its hat
their ship unravels

a yarn of how close death came to be
a shiver running diamonds down my spine

how brides compete with the sea's allure
is no secret

they hang out the wash to dry
draw water from a well

that spills
pirates steal pearls

red dye

warning   hurricane approaching
buy candles say prayers close
shutters hold hands
tight

play blindfolded
so the rain doesn't catch your fears

will Noah build his ark

will we go in pairs or one by one

will the conquistadors be there

wild oats

rumor   my brother is sowing his oats

I know better
he is burning them

with lighter fluid   playing with edges
cursing like a mad dog in heat

all this is true and more and no doubt
yes
            but still
            he is my brother

hiding in his lion suit   watching

for when I fall and scrape my knee
if I'll call his name

or pretend nothing happened

memory runs away

my mind   moth-eaten flutters
here and there

       lands on an old bus route

where they sold used books for pennies
that we couldn't afford

she'd laugh

we're lucky
we have apples in our pockets

what comes from the deep

isn't a message in a bottle

you can't catch
heave-ho

hold
            her face in your hands

fisherman know
what comes from the sea

is not returned

there's no gold
on the ocean's floor

only skeletons
sailors take for lucky charms

water stains her hands

salt makes them bitter

my abuela carries my mother's heart
up and down cobbled streets

you'd think she was a beggar
and not my grandmother

who blindfolded in her sleep before dawn
makes mouthwatering polvorones

wedding cookies with so much sugar
that for one second

the echo of my mother's voice taunting me to eat
just one just one   no más no más

simmers inside me   melts
my abuela's horse laughter

shaking the sugar box she sings

oh el polvo blanco de los sueños

ah the white dust of dreams

without leaves   trees are bare

if you fall out of the sky
stars don't catch you

gravity does

my abuela whispers

God hides in an apple
save seeds

on the day of my mother's death
I go to my room

my mouth burns calypso
I shout to the wall

my mother is a songbird spinning me free

more riddles more maize

if stars make holes in the sky when they fall
did my mother leave her knitting needles
her recipes for a sore throat

I am afraid of forgetting

her hands chattered when I coughed
her voice mixed bitter and sweet

how deep the forest is tattooed on a sailor's arm

      papa lets me keep old Christmas lights

      they blink on and off like castaway dresses
      my mother sewed for me

      they make me seasick   I wet the bed

      I wish I knew how whales lost in TV movies hear
      what echoes back

      then I'd find her song threads   make cornbread
      solve the riddle of who made the world spin

at night I hear

my grandmother polishing silver
fishermen mending their nets

Montezuma's empty bowls
sailors swaying in their sleep

my father

> I don't hear my mother's voice
> or Pedro's
> arguing back and forth
> who is right who is wrong

locked in a pirate's chest
deep beneath the ocean's red dye

> is the key to feather-making

With Thanks

I owe a debt of gratitude to my poetry teachers, past and present. Their guidance has shaped the way I listen to language and weave words together. Aaron Shurin, Norma Cole, Edward Smallfield, Arthur Sze, Genine Lentine, and Julie Bruck have each opened new doors of imagination and craft. Each left an indelible mark on my work.

This book could not exist without the encouragement, love, and generosity of my family and friends. Marie and Bill Waterman, Jane and Michael Rice, Lisa Burlini, Aline Libassi, and Roberta Mundie offered support and belief. Their belief helped carry this project from dream to completion.

I especially thank Bernard Osher for his faith in me.

I am equally indebted to the Fearless Poets—Carol Allen, Raluca Ioanid, Eli Ipp, Janette Jamison, Anne Irving, Barbara Leff, Kira Kmetz, Hannah Nguyen, Marilyn Meisenheimer, Sharanya Naik, Barbara Stevenson, Karen Sundheim, Ruth Vose, and Bridget Wagner—whose voices, courage, and companionship continue to remind me of the power of a shared creative journey.

JoAnna Scandiffio is a graduate gemologist and educator based in San Francisco. She earned her Master of Arts from the University of San Francisco and has taught at Queens College in New York City and City College of San Francisco.

Her poems are like bird nests, made with fragments randomly connected to hold the moment.

Scandiffio's work appeared in *Calyx, The Ekphrastic Review, Gyroscope Review, Ink in Thirds, Italian Americana, Poets 11, The MacGuffin, The Poeming Pigeon, The RavensPerch, Riders of the Storm, Switched-on-Gutenberg,* and other journals.

She is a Pushcart Prize Nominee and a finalist for the Jane Underwood Prize.

More of her poems can be found at joannascandiffio.com.

*9 798889 902154 *